The **WH?** Books

Aharon Shemi and Danny Kerman

WHEN

Sterling Publishing Co. Inc. New York

Series Editor: Nira Harel
Consultants: Dr. Yoram Yom-Tov
             Dr. Amos Ar
Translation: Tamar Berkowitz

10 9 8 7 6 5 4 3 2 1

© 1985 by Sterling Publishing Co., Inc.
Two Park Avenue, New York, N.Y. 10016
and by Massada Ltd., Publishers

Distributed in Canada by Oak Tree Press Ltd.
c/o Canadian Manda Group, P.O. Box 920, Station U
Toronto, Ontario, Canada M8Z 5P9

Manufactured in Israel.

ISBN 0-8069-4710-1

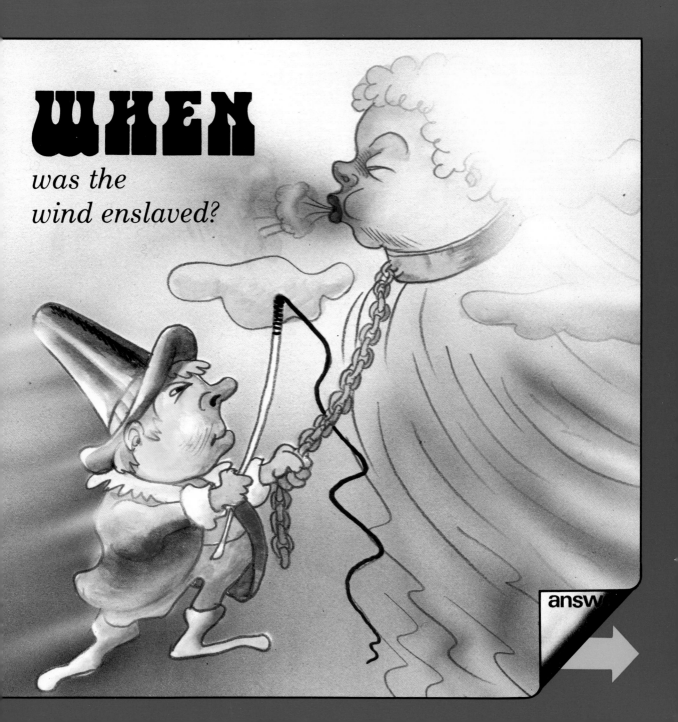

Many years ago the wind was the power source for machines and certain types of transportation. On the seas, huge ships had large sails which caught the wind and moved the ship forward. On land you could find tall narrow buildings with giant "wings" attached to them. These wings were turned slowly by the wind. In most countries, these windmills were used to grind flour.

But in Holland the windmills served another purpose. For hundreds of years the Dutch battled against the threat of floods. They used hundreds of windmills to pump out the ocean water that flooded their fields. Then the fields could be used to grow food.

Today you can still see many windmills in Holland. They remind us of the days when the Dutch people used the wind in order to save their land from the sea.

*was the
wind
enslaved?*

*does a coat
warm you?*

Never, because it's not the coat that warms you. It is your body that warms you — the coat only keeps the warmth in.

We call fur warm clothing because it keeps in the body heat better than cotton does. Why? In order for one material to keep the heat better than another it must be a good "insulator." A good insulator is something that makes it hard for heat to escape.

Air is a good insulator, as long as it is sealed in and can't move. The air between two windows insulates.

The air inside a fur coat insulates the heat of the body and makes sure that it won't escape into the cold air outside. So it's not the clothing that warms you, but your body.

WHEN
does the whale eat?

answer

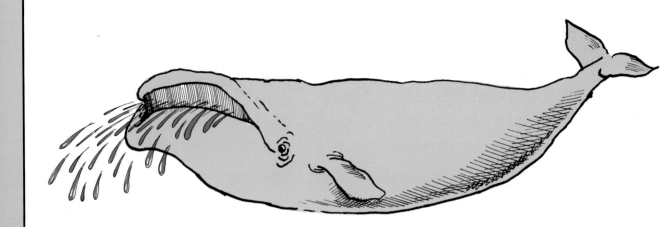

The whale has a very big mouth. In fact, about a third of the whale's body is a mouth! As the whale swims, it opens its mouth and swallows large quantities of sea water. The water is filled with millions of very tiny shrimps.

On the sides of the whale's mouth are many small bristles called baleen. With its huge tongue, the whale spews the water out, and the shrimps are trapped in these baleen. Then the whale has a hearty meal.

The whale is the largest animal on earth. Yet it doesn't use its great strength to fight for food. The whale just opens its mouth, and swallows little shrimps. That's the whale's breakfast, lunch and dinner.

WHEN

does the whale eat?

WHEN

are butterflies frightened?

Some butterflies can't really be frightened. They are so poisonous that no other animal dares to eat them. But there are other butterflies which must make themselves invisible.

Being invisible is really the only way these butterflies can protect themselves. After all, a butterfly doesn't have teeth or a sting. And it can't fly fast enough to escape.

The striped fur of tigers matches the strips of light and shade of the jungle. Many butterflies appear to vanish when they stand on a branch or the leaf of a plant.

When frightened this type of butterfly freezes in its place. Its coloring matches its surroundings. Therefore, you can't tell the difference between the butterfly and the plant. That way the butterfly can see you, but you can't see it!

A baby loves to touch everything in sight. He likes to turn things over and feel them. He likes to grab things because they make noise or smell good. Suddenly, when a baby touches a stove, he pulls his hand back quickly and cries out in pain. His finger hurts. He's been warned.

Pain is a warning signal. If the baby hadn't felt pain he would have been badly burned. It's better for a baby to cry. Sometimes our body really hurts us, like when we have a bad stomachache. This is a signal that something is wrong, and that we should do something about it. You should stop eating, and you may have to call a doctor.

Pain is not a good feeling, but we should always remember that pain is a very good warning signal.

WHEN

is pain a good warning signal?

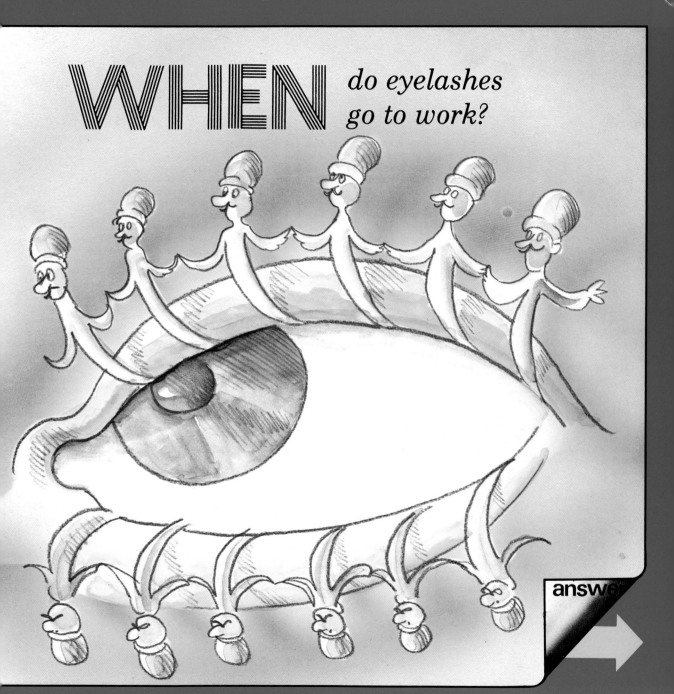

WHEN

*do eyelashes
go to work?*

If a little piece of dust falls on your hand, you hardly notice it. If a mosquito flies into your nose, you sneeze and it flies out. But what happens if a piece of dust or a mosquito gets into your eye?

Eyelashes protect one of the most important and sensitive parts of our body—our eyes. Eyelashes prevent foreign objects, such as dust and mosquitoes, from entering the eye. They don't *always* succeed. Then the eye really hurts.

WHEN

was fruit used as a medicine?

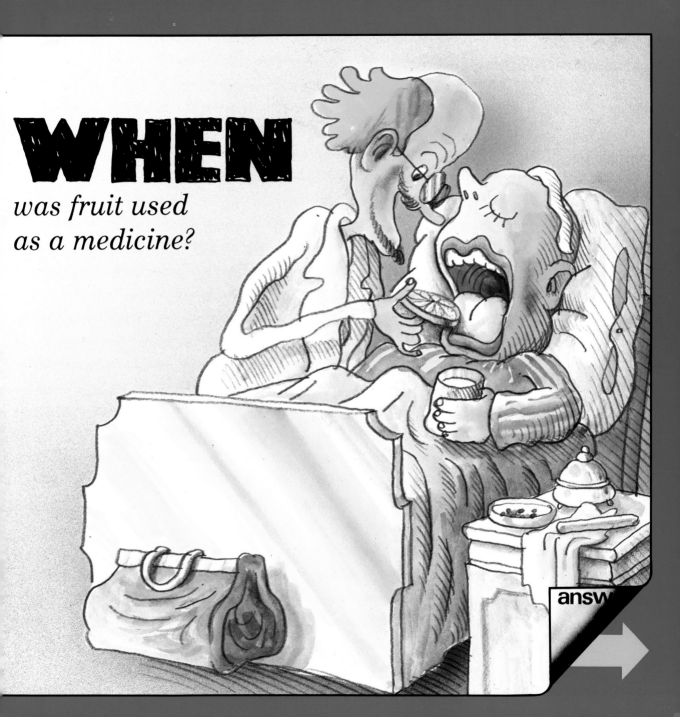

answ →

Long ago, when ships took months to sail to their destinations, there were no refrigerators. The crew could only stock food that wouldn't spoil on long voyages—preserved meat and dry bread, for example. Sometimes the sailors could eat the fish they caught at sea.

During that time, many sailors suffered from a disease called scurvy. Their hair fell out and so did their teeth. Sometimes they even died from this disease.

Then it was discovered that scurvy was brought on by the lack of fresh food—especially fruit. Sailors began to take along fresh lemons on their long journeys. From that day on, no ship sailed without a crate of lemons. The disease, scurvy, disappeared.

Today we know that lemons contain Vitamin C. You can buy this vitamin at a drug store. You can also get Vitamin C by eating lemons as well as grapefruits, oranges, and limes.

This story may also explain why people still sprinkle a few drops of lemon on their fish.

WHEN

was fruit used as a medicine?

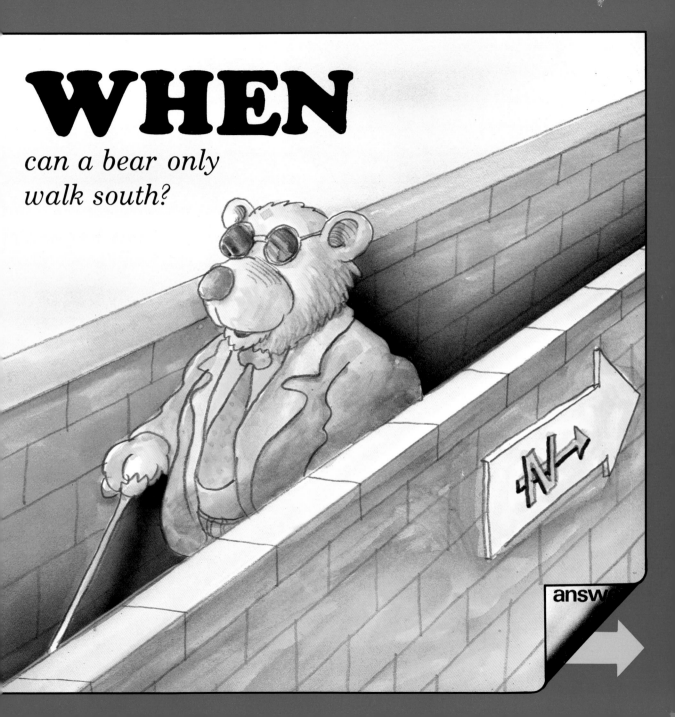

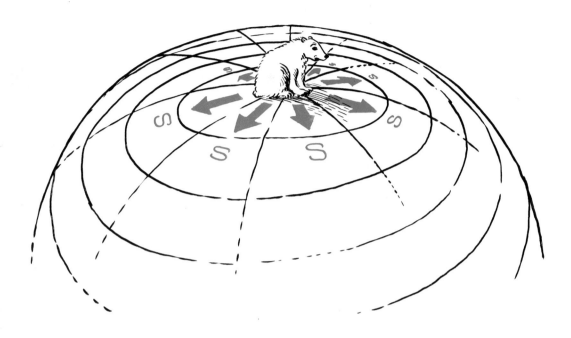

A bear can only walk southward when he is at the North Pole.

If you were to stand at the North Pole and start to walk, you could only head south. It wouldn't matter whether you moved forward, backward, or to either side. At this spot there is no east or west—only south.

Which bears live in the North Pole region? White polar bears, of course.

WHEN

can a bear only walk south?

WHEN

do bats see better than you?

answer →

Bats see the best at night. In the daytime bats can't see at all. The bat's eyes are designed to help it see at night. Too much light blinds the bat.

Our eyes, in contrast, are designed mainly for seeing in daylight. At night our vision is poorer.

But the cat's eyes are made for seeing both in the day and at night. The cat's pupils widen a great deal at night and become very narrow in daylight. When the pupil expands, a greater amount of light will enter the eye. Then the cat can see at night. And when the pupil contracts, the cat's eyes are protected against the bright daylight.

That's so the cat won't become like the bat, who can only see at night.

WHEN

do bats see better than you?

WHEN

do elephants start walking?

answe →

Only a few hours have passed since the elephant calf was born. Look, he's already standing on his legs and beginning to walk. Elephants eat a lot of food to keep alive. To find this food, they have to walk all the time. If the baby elephant had to wait a year before starting to walk, the way human babies do, elephants would die of starvation.

When do gazelles start walking? A newborn gazelle can stand up only two hours after it is born. Gazelles are born in the field. They have to be able to run in case a hungry animal approaches.

The newborn fox pup can afford to take his time. He hides inside the den where his mother gave birth to him. He starts to walk when he's five weeks old.

The kangaroo joey takes about six months. He's very tiny when he's born. His mother carries him around in her pouch until he's big enough to get around on his own. But this wouldn't be a very good system for the mother elephant!

WHEN

do elephants start walking?

WHEN

answ

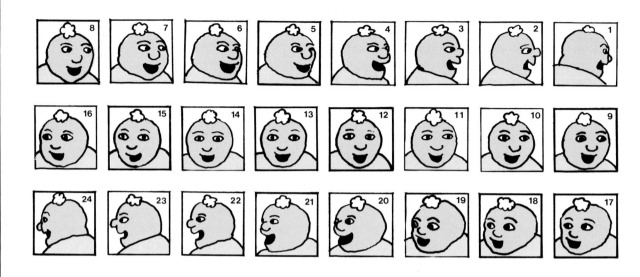

The pictures on the film of a movie always stand still. They never move.

The movement we see on the screen is caused by the way the still pictures are shown to us. Every movie film is made up of a series of pictures that don't move. Each picture is only a little different from the one before it.

The projector moves the pictures and shows them one after the other, at a speed of 24 pictures a second. Our eyes do not see the machine moving the film from one picture to the next, because it does this very quickly. When the 24 pictures (above) are shown, what you see on the movie screen is a person turning his head—in one second. Each picture shown is only part of the motion, in this case, 1/24 of it.

And how long is a second? A second is the time it take you to say "they never move."

WHEN

do the movies stop moving?